M000117541

I WOULD DO ANYTHING FOR LOAF

I Would Do Anything for Loaf

Tom Alario & Kristen Greska

gatekeeper press™

Columbus, Ohio

I Would Do Anything for Loaf
Published by Gatekeeper Press
2167 Stringtown Rd, Suite 109
Columbus, OH 43123-2989
www.GatekeeperPress.com

Library of Congress Control Number: 2020950235

ISBN (hardcover): 9781662907234
eISBN: 9781662907241

Contents

FOREWORD

Cooking has become — scratch that — *life* has become tedious, frustrating, and often more of a dreaded chore than we would like it to be. Enjoying our food has become lost in the hectic modern zeitgeist. This book is as much a cookbook as people who use the word *zeitgeist* are intellectuals — partly.

This book started as a silly idea that neither of us thought would become a reality. However, as we found ourselves with not much else to do, being quarantined during the COVID-19 pandemic of 2020, the silly idea just kept expanding before our eyes. The world around us seemed to be getting darker, but we did notice that people everywhere were being inspired by the sudden forced shift in priorities. People were taking a newfound interest in things like breadmaking and sewing, and in doing so, were finding ways to stay purposeful and involved with society. Despite the hardships, this time really did provide many of us the opportunity to refocus our energy away from the hustle and bustle.

The journey of creating this content was a celebration of our own creativity, and even that less-traveled path was borne of a willingness to say "yes" to being playful. On a date night, we decided to make a meatloaf but with a twist. We joked about having a "loaf of the month"! From there the play became easy; our imaginations were wide open and wild. The specifics of how we developed this book are inconsequential to your experiencing it, as long as it is understood that we had invigorated the spirit of play into something

that has sadly and unfortunately gone toward the mundane, the bland, the commodified, the "set it and forget it" soulless: home-cooked meals.

While meatloaf was typically a meal designed for a tired parent trying to whip up something quick and cheap for the family, the ideas in this book are meant for a little more than that. Yes, this is a collection of recipes in its structure, but we hope it also serves as an inspiration to make a bonding experience out of cooking. We are neither trained chefs nor trained authors! With a shared passion for cooking (and being ridiculous), we tapped into a sustained creative vein. Getting to eat good food was a small bonus. The real benefit was bonding like neither of us imagined we would.

All of our loaves were named with our love of puns and music in mind, so scan this QR code for a specially curated playlist!

WHAT DO I NEED TO BEGIN?

As long as the wheels are turning, as long as the fires are burning, as long as your dreams are coming true, you're probably on the right path towards making a meatloaf.

In fact, most of the loaf components are probably things you already have around the kitchen. Remember that one time you bought Worcestershire sauce and it's been sitting on the fridge door for five years? You're going to use it now.

During each loaf's conception stage, we used a super bare-bones outline for what we considered the hallmark of a meatloaf. Here is a skeleton shopping list of items you will need.*

- **Meat**: You'll need about 2 lbs of any ground meat.
- **Egg**: One is enough (one egg *is* an oeuf, if you remember your French lessons).
- **Milk**: Most recipes will require about a half-cup of milk or some kind of creamy component.
- **Bread crumbs**: You can use actual bread crumbs or anything crumbled that will absorb moisture and help bind your meat and filling.
- **Vegetables**: Cooked or not, you're going to want some chopped vegetables in the loaf for crunch and flavor. Most common are things like onion, celery, carrots, and garlic.
- **Herbs**: You can use fresh or dried.
- **Spices**: Just go for it.

- **Ketchup**: Any tomato- or red pepper-based sauce works well in this role.
- **Worcestershire**: This is also easily substituted with other sauces.
- **Salt and pepper**: PUSH IT ... to taste.

In writing these recipes, we are assuming that you have some pretty basic kitchen tools. If we used something wild and crazy to make our loaf, we will be sure to point that out in the foreword of each recipe so you don't feel like a dumbass for not just having a meat grinder lying around.

Here are some gold standards of kitchen tools you will need:

- **Hands**: Nature's spoons.
- **Measuring cups/measuring spoons:** Or eyeballs if your superpower is "units of measure." **
- **Large mixing bowl:** Keep in mind, you're using about 6 cups of total ingredients when it's all said and done, so you'll want a bowl that can hold that *and* offer room so that all the loafy goodness isn't spilling out over the edge.
- **Sauté pan:** For cooking your vegetables.
- **Bread/Loaf pan**: A standard pan is **8½ x 4½ and is 2½ inches deep**. If you didn't bring your tape measure to the store, it looks like the size of a loaf of bread. Get that one.

Now here's where you can start to get creative because, of course, there are different types of pans, and each of them will offer a slight variation on how your loaf cooks through. Some are metal, some are ceramic, some are porcelain, some are lamb-shaped. The best thing, in our opinion, is to try different pans made of different materials and see what end product you like best. We tend to lean towards the porcelain pans because they seem to hold and distribute heat the best. Any pan will do, and you'll see throughout this book that we do experiment with some unusual pan shapes!

- **Oven**: There's no getting around this ... you need a heat source to cook your meatloaf. This seems like a joke inclusion to the list of "things you need," but it's important to talk about how not all ovens are created equal. We're not saying you need to go out and get a better oven; there are just things to consider. The cooking time absolutely depends on your particular oven. Our recipes were written based on what we know of our oven and its capabilities. You may not have to cook your meatloaves as long as we do, or you might find that you need to cook them longer.

Which brings us to the next need ....

- **Meat thermometer**: We do not recommend cooking meat without a means of taking the internal temperature. Your meatloaf should be fully cooked. A quick note on using the thermometer if you've never used one before: Insert the metal prong into the thickest part of the loaf, about halfway in (if you remember our measurements of a standard pan, we're talking 1¼ inch deep). Keep the thermometer inserted until it stops increasing the reading. Be careful not to take the temperature too close to the bottom or sides of the pan because you will be getting the temperature of the vessel and not the loaf itself.

At this point you should be ready to try your hand at making a meatloaf. This is the fun part! We encourage you to try our recipes, but also get creative if the spirit moves you. We don't take ourselves or our loaves too seriously, and we've found that as long as you're having fun cooking, you're probably going to churn out a bomb-ass loaf.

Now quit loafin' around! Go make some meatloaf!

*Secret: When you get to the "Loafin' on a Prayer" recipe, it's just a regular old meatloaf, if that's all you feel like making.

**Someone PLEASE make a superhero comic about Units of Measure Man.

LOAF IN THE THAI(M) OF COVID

THE THAI LOAF

s mentioned previously, this entire book was written amidst the global coronavirus pandemic that all but ruined the year 2020.* We took our downtime and decided to create something that brought us joy — something we could share with others, and something that would last in our family for years to come.

Love inspired this book. The Thai culture and cuisine inspired this loaf. Communal dining is very common in Thailand; these are big family meals where you eat with your hands and just spend time with those you love. We hope that when you make this loaf, everyone sits down together, turns off the devices and TVs, and talks to one another. Talk about what happened to the world in 2020. Listen to one another. Try to understand a different perspective. Oh — and enjoy the meatloaf!

So maybe 2020 didn't get ruined after all. Maybe the "new normal" gave us the opportunity to create a book that we may have otherwise been too busy to dedicate time to.

Ingredients:

- 1 lb pork
- 1 lb chicken
- 4 oz Thai red curry paste
- 1 tsp dried Thai basil
- ¼ c coconut milk
- 1 red pepper — diced
- ½ yellow onion — diced
- 2 small carrots — diced
- 2 tbsp shredded ginger
- 1 tbsp fresh basil
- zest from ½ a lime
- 2 tbsp peanut sauce
- 1 egg
- 1 ¼ cup panko breadcrumbs
- ¼ tsp garlic powder
- ¼ tsp salt
- ¼ tsp pepper
- ¼ tsp sesame seeds
- 3 tbsp sweet chili sauce for topping

Recipe:

- Preheat oven to 350, grease 5x9 loaf pan with sesame oil or butter.
- Sauté red pepper, onion, carrot, and ginger.
- In large bowl, mix by hand pork and chicken.
- Add in Thai red curry paste, fresh basil, dried Thai basil, lime zest, coconut milk, and peanut sauce. Mix until well combined.
- Stir in sautéed veggies, garlic powder, salt, pepper, and sesame seeds.
- Crack in egg at room temperature. Top with panko and mix well.
- Bake for 55 minutes at 350º F.
- Check internal temperature to be 160º F.
- Let sit for 15 minutes before slicing to serve.

We topped the loaf with sweet chili sauce and served it with jasmine rice and sautéed sugar snap peas.

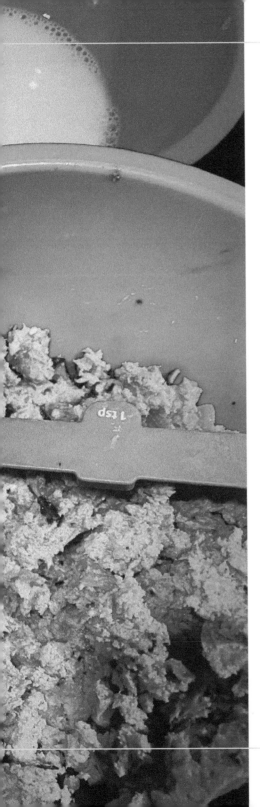

he idea for "loaftovers" came when we realized that one meatloaf for two people is a hell of an undertaking to eat. We basically figured we would be eating the same meal for a week straight just to not let anything spoil. It dawned on us that we could, in fact, get creative with what was left after we had had our fill of the loaf. Not every meatloaf had a loaftover component, but most of them did. You will see ideas for loaftovers sprinkled in with the recipe pages, but honestly, they are pretty much all interchangeable. After the *Livin' La Vida Loaf-a*, we made baked nachos with all the ingredients. You really could do that with any of the loaves. One of the cool things we noted was that just about every cuisine style has some kind of "dumpling," be it steamed or boiled or fried. Every single one of these could be reborn as a "dumpling" child to the parent loaf. Our loaftovers, as with everything in this book, are just suggestions and what we decided to do with the remaining loaf filling.

We aren't going to share full-build recipes for each loaftover because each of these is a pretty simple remix of the loaf that you *do* have the recipe for. We hope that you are inspired to try your own loaftover recipes as well!

The first loaftover is the reincarnation of *Loaf in the Thai(m) of COVID*. We had about three thick slices of the loaf left and a packet of wonton wrappers from the grocery store; you do the math. Nothing was added to the leftover loaf mixture to create these sweet little dumplings.

SAUSAGE PEPPERS LOAFLY HEARTS CLUB BAND

The Italian Loaf

ausage Peppers was the first loaf we made together. We had decided to make a meatloaf, and while shopping for ingredients, we came to the realization that we didn't need to follow a traditional recipe. We saw that the store had uncased Italian sausage and the ideas snowballed from there. What do you think of when you think "Italian sausage"? For us it was the classic Italian sausage sandwich: sautéed peppers and onions, mixed with a little marinara and served on a thick, toasted roll. Because this was the first loaf, it has a special place in our hearts, so we hope you will enjoy the show!

Ingredients:

- 1 lb ground round
- 1 lb ground Italian sausage
- 1 green pepper — diced
- 1 onion — diced
- 2 tbsp stone-ground mustard
- 2 tbsp dried oregano
- 3 cloves of garlic — minced
- 1 tsp fennel seeds
- 1 roll stale or toasted Italian bread — hand-pulled to 1-inch pieces
- ½ c Italian breadcrumbs
- 1 egg
- 1 c milk
- salt and pepper to taste
- pasta sauce
- shredded mozzarella

Recipe:

- Preheat oven to 350º F.; grease 5x9 loaf pan with butter or olive oil.
- Sauté green pepper, onion, and garlic in a small pan over medium heat. Cool to room temperature.
- In large bowl, mix by hand beef, sausage, and sautéed veggies.
- Add in mustard, oregano, fennel seeds, and milk. Mix until well combined.
- Crack in egg at room temperature. Top with breadcrumbs and bread chunks, and mix until well combined.
- Bake for 40 minutes at 350º F. Top with tomato sauce and shredded mozzarella cheese.
- Bake for another 20 minutes. Check internal temp to be at least 160º F.
- Let sit for 15 minutes before slicing to serve.

The loaftover? You guessed it … ravioli. We did make our own pasta and it was an all-day effort, but totally worth it.

LIVIN' LA VIDA LOAF-A

THE MEXICAN LOAF

*I*t's not often that anything makes you want to take your clothes off and go dancing in the rain, but this loaf might come pretty darn close. This loaf was lovingly called "the taco loaf" during its conception. We basically wanted everything you love about a taco dinner in one neat slice of meatloaf. This was the first loaf where we started to think outside the bun in terms of breadcrumbs. Up until now we had just been using different types of breadcrumbs; this time we got creative and crushed up some tortilla chips that gave our new loaf a nice crunch! Dancing around the kitchen to Ricky Martin radio while you make this isn't required, but it is highly recommended.

Ingredients:

- 1½ lbs ground beef
- ½ lb ground chorizo
- 1 onion — diced
- 1 poblano pepper — diced
- ¾ c corn (canned or fresh)
- 1½ tsp taco seasoning
- 2 tbsp chopped cilantro
- 2 tbsp mole + 2 tbsp mole for topping
- 1 tbsp salsa verde
- 1 shot tequila*
- ½ tsp lime juice
- ½ c crema
- 1 egg
- 1 c crushed tortilla chips (in food processor for a finer grind)
- ¼ c Chihuahua cheese

One shot for the loaf. At least one shot for the chef(s). Please loaf responsibly.

Recipe:

- Preheat oven to 350° F.; grease 5x9 loaf pan with butter.
- Sauté onion and poblano pepper in a small pan over medium heat. Cool to room temperature.
- In large bowl, mix by hand beef, chorizo, corn, cilantro, and sautéed veggies.
- Add in taco seasoning, mole, salsa verde, tequila, lime juice, and crema. Mix until well combined.
- Crack in egg at room temperature. Top with crushed tortilla chips and mix well.
- Bake for 50 minutes at 350° F. Top with mole and Chihuahua cheese.
- Bake for another 10 minutes. Check internal temperature to be 160° F.
- Let sit for 15 minutes before slicing to serve.

We served with rice and beans, guac, and shredded lettuce.

The loaftover for this was a no-brainer. We had just enough of all the ingredients to make a huge pile of baked nachos. Eaten so quickly; not pictured. You know what nachos look like.

Greeced Loafnin'

The Greek Loaf

pa! This loaf took its inspiration from Mediterranean cuisine; using lamb, mint, red peppers, olives, and feta. It was the perfect mix of savory, bright, and salty. We also learned some important lessons about what kinds of alcohol you can set on fire to make flaming cheese. Turns out, not many will light on fire, but they will all get you drunk.

Ingredients:

- 1 lb ground beef
- 1 lb ground lamb
- 1 red onion — roughly chopped
- 1 jar pickled roasted red peppers — roughly chopped
- ⅓ c black olives — sliced
- 1 c spinach — roughly chopped
- 1 tbsp fresh mint leaves
- 1 tbsp fresh dill
- ¼ c goat cheese
- ½ c tzatziki sauce
- 1 tbsp tahini
- 2 tbsp red pepper paste
- 1 tbsp black pepper
- 1 egg
- 2 oven-roasted pitas — ground in food processor

Optional:
kefalotyri cheese slices for saganaki

Recipe:

- Preheat oven to 350º F.; grease 5x9 loaf pan with butter.
- Place onion, red peppers, black olives, spinach, mint, dill, and goat cheese in a food processor. Process until finely chopped and well mixed.
- In large bowl, mix by hand beef, lamb, and chopped veggies.
- Add in tahini, red pepper paste, black pepper, and tzatziki sauce. Mix until well combined.
- Crack in egg at room temperature. Top with crushed pita bread and mix well.
- Bake for 55 minutes at 350º F.
- Check internal temp to be 160º F.
- Let sit for 15 minutes before slicing to serve.

Optional:
Top with slice of saganaki.

We served with spanakorizo and Greek salad.

Spanakorizo (Greek Rice)

he loaftover used the loaf and the rice side dish, so we are including the recipe for the spanakorizo. This unique type of dumpling is called a dolma. It's ground meat and rice wrapped in pickled grape leaves and boiled. Grape leaves are easy to come by in most supermarkets. The key is to wash them first to dilute some of their sourness. Don't overfill your dolma because the leaves will unravel if not tightly wrapped. Keep them submerged in the pot with a heavy plate while they simmer themselves into deliciousness.

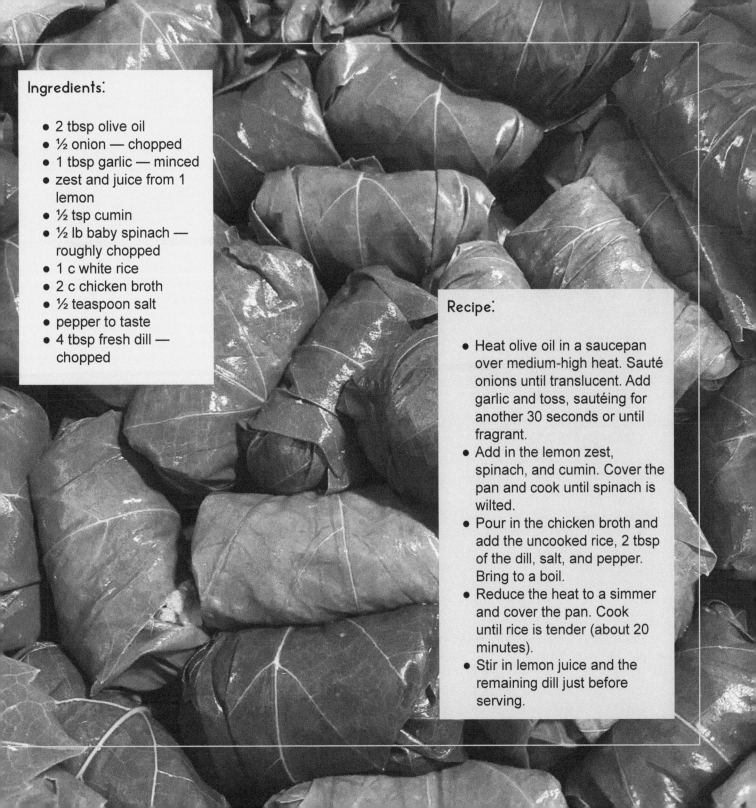

Ingredients:

- 2 tbsp olive oil
- ½ onion — chopped
- 1 tbsp garlic — minced
- zest and juice from 1 lemon
- ½ tsp cumin
- ½ lb baby spinach — roughly chopped
- 1 c white rice
- 2 c chicken broth
- ½ teaspoon salt
- pepper to taste
- 4 tbsp fresh dill — chopped

Recipe:

- Heat olive oil in a saucepan over medium-high heat. Sauté onions until translucent. Add garlic and toss, sautéing for another 30 seconds or until fragrant.
- Add in the lemon zest, spinach, and cumin. Cover the pan and cook until spinach is wilted.
- Pour in the chicken broth and add the uncooked rice, 2 tbsp of the dill, salt, and pepper. Bring to a boil.
- Reduce the heat to a simmer and cover the pan. Cook until rice is tender (about 20 minutes).
- Stir in lemon juice and the remaining dill just before serving.

oooooaaaahhhh … we're halfway there ….

We're gonna admit that this isn't the first time in this book where we get a little "extra." Most of these loaves are pretty simple to make. Some of them are just monstrosities, and we would be thrilled and honored if anyone else took the time to be as ridiculous as we felt making the extravagant loaves. As extra as this loaf is, it is actually just a regular old meatloaf, akin to what you might remember your mom making. So if you want a classic meatloaf, just don't shape it like a GD lamb*.

It was Easter Sunday in the Greskalario household. It seemed like a perfect time to pull out the old lamb cake pans and try to make a meatloaf with them! Apparently lamb cake for Easter is not a ubiquitous tradition, but if it was for you then you're going to love this wild idea. This loaf will absolutely take you all day to make because in order to "ice" it (with potatoes), the loaf needs to be pretty cold; otherwise it will melt the potatoes right off — same principle as icing a cake. The good news is that you'll have plenty of time to make the potatoes while the loaf chills, or, like, hang out with your family hunting for eggs, if that's a thing you do.

Ingredients:

For the loaf
- 1 lb ground beef
- 1 lb ground pork
- 1 green pepper — diced
- 1 onion — diced
- 1 carrot — diced
- 2 cloves of garlic — minced
- 1 tsp thyme
- 1 tsp paprika
- 2 tbsp chili sauce or ketchup
- 1 tbsp Worcestershire sauce
- 1 c breadcrumbs**
- 1 egg
- 1 c milk
- salt and pepper to taste
- whatever veggies you have lying around for facial features! We used black beans and tomato.

For the duchess potatoes
- 3 lbs russet potatoes, peeled and chopped into 1-inch cubes
- 1 tbsp salt
- 1¼ c shredded white Cheddar
- ⅓ c heavy cream
- ⅛ tsp ground nutmeg
- ¼ tsp white pepper
- 4 large egg yolks
- 4 tbsp melted butter

Recipe:

- Preheat oven to 350º F.
- Grease both sides of a lamb-shaped cake pan with butter.
- Sauté green pepper, onion, carrot, and garlic in a small pan over medium heat. Cool to room temperature.
- In large bowl, mix by hand beef, pork, and sautéed veggies.
- Add in thyme, paprika, chili sauce, Worcestershire sauce, and milk. Mix until well combined.
- Crack in egg at room temperature. Top with breadcrumbs and mix well by hand.
- Bake for 45 minutes at 350º F. Check internal temperature to be 160º F.
- Remove from the oven, bring to room temperature, and then chill in the refrigerator for at least 2 hours.

While chilling, make the **duchess potatoes.**

For the potatoes:

- Place the peeled potato chunks in a large sauce pot and cover with water and a pinch of salt. Bring water to a boil and simmer until the potatoes are fork-tender.
- Drain the water from the potatoes and let dry for a few minutes.
- Return the potatoes to the pot over medium heat.
- Stir in the shredded cheese, cream, nutmeg, and white pepper.
- Blend the potatoes until smooth.
- Temper the eggs with a tiny bit of the mashed potatoes so they don't cook, then quickly stir the yolks into the potato mixture.

For this loaf you will need a lamb-shaped cake pan and an icing piping bag with tips. If you're not inclined to be that fancy, you can use a large freezer bag with a corner cut out to decorate your lamb.

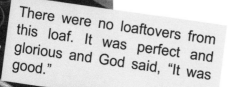

There were no loaftovers from this loaf. It was perfect and glorious and God said, "It was good."

Back to the loaf:

- Preheat oven to 400° F.
- Carefully remove each half of the meatloaf from the form pans. Spread a thin layer of duchess potatoes on one half to stick them together. Stand the monster up. **The head will fall off. Be prepared to prop that bad boy up with, like, a carrot or some twigs.**
- Fill a pastry bag with the duchess potatoes and pipe in the shape of a cute, fluffy lamb of god.
- Brush the son of man with melted butter.
- Bake again on lowest rack for 20 minutes to brown and firm the potatoes.
- Add on some eyes ... and don't forget those juicy red lips.

**I'm only a little bit ashamed to admit that I bought Eucharist wafers (if you're not Catholic, google it) on Amazon and popped that in the food processor, and THAT'S what was used as breadcrumbs. If you're not feeling sacrilegious, just use breadcrumbs. And please, for the loaf of God, don't be mad at me. Honestly, it doesn't make a difference if you use it or not.

Love, Kristen (Tom declined to be party to this decision)

THAT LOAF IS HOISIN

THE JAPANESE LOAF

This is a blend of beef and pork, traditional Asian spices, and sauces, reminiscent of gyoza filling. Coconut milk, lemongrass, ginger, and Chinese five spice really transform what could easily be a standard meatloaf. We used a lemongrass paste that we found at a local supermarket, but when we remade this loaf visiting some family out of town, we were unable to find lemongrass paste and pretty much everyone looked at us like we were crazy. We are, but that's beside the point. We did, however, find it available for purchase online, and there are recipes to make your own. It's not the most important part of the loaf, but it definitely enhances the Asian flavor.

Ingredients:

- 1½ lbs ground pork
- ½ lb ground beef
- 1 onion — diced
- 2 carrots — diced
- 1 baby bok choy — roughly chopped
- 2 cloves of garlic — minced
- 1 tbsp fresh ginger — minced
- 1 bunch green onion
- 1 tsp lemongrass paste
- ¼ tsp Chinese five spice
- ¼ tsp black pepper
- 1 tbsp soy sauce
- 1 c coconut milk
- ¼ c Katsu sauce
- 1 egg
- 1 c panko breadcrumbs
- ¼ c hoisin sauce
- 1 tbsp sesame seeds
- wasabi on the side*

Recipe:

- Preheat oven to 350º F.; grease 5x9 loaf pan with butter or coconut oil.
- Sauté bok choy, onion, ginger, and garlic in a small pan over medium heat. Sauté until bok choy is wilted. Cool to room temperature.
- In large bowl, mix by hand pork, beef, fresh green onion, and the sautéed veggies.
- Add in lemongrass paste, Chinese five spice, pepper, soy, coconut milk, and Katsu. Mix until well combined.
- Crack in egg at room temperature. Top with panko and mix well by hand.
- Bake for 40 minutes at 350º F. Top with hoisin and sprinkle with sesame seeds.
- Bake for another 20 minutes. Check internal temp to be 160º F.
- Let sit for 15 minutes before slicing to serve.

We served it with white rice and roasted broccoli.

Serve with a dollop of wasabi ... but if I were you, I'd take precaution.

The loaftovers? More dumplings. Duh ... mplings.

all me Ishmael, because this loaf is our Moby Dick. We had such high hopes for making a splash with this one, but it was just a wreck. We made the decision to include the "recipe" (i.e., what *we* did and failed at) to share with you despite this not turning out like we had hoped or planned, as it was still part of the creative process. This may have been the first loaf where we didn't have fun making it, and that probably showed in the finished product. We were both tired but had planned to try this one and pushed through even though we should have rested. It actually took us quite a while after making this flop before diving (see what I did there?) back into the world of meatloaf. We were shook. Until this one, they had all been amazing hits. The best thing to come out of this project were the "crab cakes" we made with the remaining loaf mixture. Those were killer. There were no photos taken of the loaf in question (or the loaftover crab cakes for that matter). There is no record of it having existed — just this idea. Let this be a lesson to all of you; rest when your body tells you to rest. No good will come of forcing yourself to do something because you think you have to.*

Not Pictured

LOAF ON THE WATER

THE SEAFOOD LOAF

Ingredients:

- 24 oz lump crab meat
- 14¾ oz canned salmon
- 6 oz canned tiny shrimp
- zest of a whole lemon
- half a lemon
- 2 tbsp tartar sauce
- 2 tbsp cocktail sauce
- 1 tbsp tarragon — chopped
- 1 shallot — diced
- 1 red onion — diced
- ¼ c green onion — chopped
- 3 ribs of celery — diced
- 3 small sweet red peppers — diced
- 1 tsp black pepper
- 1 tsp Old Bay
- 1 tsp salt
- 2 eggs
- 1½ c Ritz crackers pulsed in the food processor (¼ c set aside)

Recipe:

- Preheat oven to 400º F.; grease 5x9 loaf pan with butter.
- Sauté red peppers, celery, red onion, and shallots until just cooked.
- Strain juices from your cans of fish and mix together.
- Add in sautéed vegetables.
- Mix in raw green onions and chopped tarragon.
- Stir in lemon zest, lemon juice, tartar sauce, cocktail sauce, black pepper, salt, and Old Bay.
- Drop in two eggs and 1¼ c of crushed Ritz crackers. Mix well by hand.
- Bake for 40 min at 400º F. Top with remaining Ritz crackers and about 2 tbsp melted butter.
- Bake for another 10 minutes.
- Let sit for 15 minutes.
- Make the decision to make crab cakes with it or throw it away. Either way, top it with a white wine lemon-butter sauce.

Side note: If you happen to make a (or this) seafood loaf and it turns out to be a hit, please let us know! We would love to hear your experience!

THE MEATLOAF SANDWICH

AN INTERLUDE

We've talked a lot about the various loaftover ideas, and we thought it bore mentioning that the greatest loaftover of all time is the meatloaf sandwich. It's as timeless as the meatloaf itself. However you want to dress it, every single one of our loaves works as a meatloaf sandwich.

Meatloaf was a dish that was basically a leftover. Whatever extra "stuff" you had laying around in the fridge was probably going to end up in your meatloaf. It's likely that everyone grew up with a different kind of meatloaf recipe based on what was commonly left over in their households.

Not expected to be featured on any fine-dining menu, the meatloaf has remained a kitschy and nostalgic meal, reminding us of simpler, scrappier times.

BREAKFAST AT LOAFANY'S

THE BREAKFAST LOAF

Who said you can't have meatloaf for breakfast? Or breakfast for dinner? This one breaks all the meal rules! This pork sausage loaf is stuffed with onions, peppers, pancakes, scrambled eggs, and topped with black pepper gravy. We made it for dinner and then also ate it for breakfast the next day. I think … we both kinda liked it.

Ingredients:

For the loaf:

- 1 lb pork and fennel sausage*
- 1 lb ground chicken
- 1 green pepper — diced
- 1 onion — diced
- 3 scrambled eggs
- 1 tbsp maple syrup
- 1 tbsp Bloody Mary mix
- 1 tsp ground sage
- 1 tsp ground black pepper
- ½ tsp salt
- ¼ c buttermilk
- 2 c chopped pancake
- splash of hot sauce for topping

For the gravy:

- drippings from the loaf
- 2 tbsp butter
- 2 tbsp all-purpose flour
- 1 c heavy whipping cream
- salt and pepper to taste, but definitely like ¼ c of pepper

Recipe:

For the loaf:

- Preheat oven to 350º F.; grease 5x9 loaf pan with butter or olive oil.
- Sauté green pepper, onion, and garlic in a small pan over medium heat. Cool to room temperature.
- In large bowl, mix by hand chicken, sausage, and sautéed veggies.
- Add in syrup, Bloody Mary mix, scrambled eggs, and buttermilk. Mix until well combined.
- Crack in egg at room temperature. Top with chopped pancakes and mix until well combined.
- Bake for 40 minutes at 350º F. Top with hot sauce.
- Bake for another 20 minutes. Check internal temperature to be at least 160º F.
- Let sit for 15 minutes before slicing to serve.

For the gravy:

- While the loaf is cooling, drain the fat from the loaf into a skillet on high.
- Add butter and wait for it to become frothy.
- Whisk in 2 tbsp of flour.
- Add in heavy cream and whisk constantly until flour is incorporated and gravy is smooth.
- Once gravy is boiling, reduce temperature to a simmer and continue to whisk.
- Add in salt and pepper to taste.

We served the loaf topped with white gravy, with a side of roasted red potatoes.

We made our own pork sausage. For the adventurous loafer, you'll need a meat grinder. If you're not feeling adventurous, any ground pork breakfast sausage will do. If you use links, just make sure to squeeze the meat out of the casings.

Remember when we said sometimes we were going to be "extra"?

OH. MY. GOD. Becky, look at that loaf. If you were hoping for an Instagram-worthy meatloaf, then get McCited. This one was inspired by ... the time-honored tradition of making gigantic hamburgers, obviously. After all, what is a meatloaf but a rectangular hamburger? There will be no loaftovers with this one, we promise.

Ingredients:

For the loaf:

- 2 lb ground chuck
- 3 tbsp "special sauce"
- 1 tbsp French dressing
- 1 tbsp Worcestershire sauce
- ½ c milk
- 1 egg
- 2 tsp onion powder
- 1 tsp ground mustard
- 1 tsp ground black pepper
- ½ tsp salt
- 1 c unseasoned breadcrumbs

For the presentation:

- 1 single giant bun
- 8 slices of American cheese
- ½ c "special sauce"
- 1½ c shredded romaine lettuce

Recipe:

- Prepare ahead the "special sauce" and the single giant bun (recipes can be found just after this recipe).
- Preheat oven to 350º F.; place cake pan in oven while preheating and making the loaf.
- In large bowl, mix by hand beef and dry seasonings.
- Add in liquid components and mix well.
- Crack in egg at room temperature. Top with breadcrumbs and mix well.
- Bake for 35-40 minutes at 350º F. Check internal temperature to be at least 160º F.
- Let sit for 15 minutes before doing anything else. Don't turn off the oven!
- Place the bottom bun on a sheet pan; top with the cooled beef patty.
- Arrange American cheese slices on the patty and put back in the oven until cheese is melted (approximately 8 minutes); also put the top bun on an oven grate to warm up.
- Remove from the oven and spread "special sauce" on top of the cheese. Top with shredded lettuce and the top bun.

We served the loaf sliced like a pie with fries!

Single Giant Bun
Ingredients:

- 1 (¼-ounce) packet active dry yeast
- 3½ c pound all-purpose flour or as needed, divided
- 1 c warm water
- 1 large egg
- 3 tbsp butter — melted
- 3 tbsp white sugar
- 1¼ tsp salt
- 1 tsp olive oil
- 1 egg — beaten
- 1 tablespoon milk
- 1 tsp sesame seeds, or as needed

To make the bun:

- Line a 9-inch round cake pan with parchment paper.
- Place yeast into the bowl of a large stand mixer; whisk in ½ cup flour and warm water until smooth. Let stand until mixture is foamy, 10 to 15 minutes.
- Whisk 1 egg, melted butter, sugar, and salt thoroughly into the yeast mixture. Add remaining flour (about 3 cups).
- Fit a dough hook onto the stand mixer and knead the dough on low speed until soft and sticky, 5 to 6 minutes. Scrape sides if needed. Poke and prod the dough with a silicone spatula; if large amounts of dough stick to the spatula, add a little more flour.
- Transfer dough onto a floured work surface; dough will be sticky and elastic but not stick to your fingers. Form the dough lightly into a smooth, round shape, gently tucking loose ends underneath.
- Wipe out the stand mixer bowl, drizzle olive oil into the bowl, and turn dough over in the bowl several times to coat the surface thinly with oil. Cover bowl with aluminum foil. Let dough rise in a warm place until doubled, about 2 hours.
- Transfer dough to a floured work surface and pat to flatten bubbles and roll until smooth. Form the entire ball into a round shape, gently tucking ends underneath as before.
- Use your hands to gently pat and stretch the dough into a flat disc that fits into the cake pan, about ½ inch thick. Dust bun very lightly with flour. Drape a piece of plastic wrap over the cake pan (do not seal tightly). Let the bun rise until doubled, about 1 hour.
- Preheat the oven to 375º F.
- Beat 1 egg with milk in a small bowl, using a fork, until mixture is thoroughly combined. Very gently and lightly brush the top of the bun with egg wash without deflating the risen dough. Sprinkle bun with sesame seeds.
- Bake in the preheated oven until lightly browned on top, 20 minutes or until the top is a golden brown. Let cool completely and slice in half crosswise to serve.

"Special Sauce"

Ingredients:

- ½ c mayonnaise
- 3 tbsp French dressing
- 4 tsp sweet pickle relish
- 1 tbsp minced white onion
- 1 tsp white wine vinegar
- 1 tsp sugar
- ⅛ tsp salt

To make special sauce:

- Combine all ingredients into a bowl. Mix well.
- Let sit covered in the fridge for a few hours, or overnight preferably.
- Mix well before serving.

LOAFIN' ON THE VEG

THE VEGAN LOAF

*W*e're seeing things in a different way, and we wanted to try and make an entirely vegan loaf — a Neatloaf, if you will*. This was a particularly fun venture because the beauty of there being no raw meat meant that we could sample the flavors as we went along. We definitely didn't intend for this to taste or feel like a meat substitute; this was intended to be its own entity. The best part of this loaf was the variety of loaftovers we were able to come up with! Those didn't stay entirely vegan, but I'm sure that's no surprise.

***You will.**

Ingredients:

- 1 c brown lentils — dry
- 1 can black beans — drained and rinsed
- 2 ribs of celery
- 1 medium carrot
- ½ white onion
- ⅓ c shiitake mushroom caps — diced
- ⅛ c chopped walnuts
- 2 cloves of garlic
- 1 c instant oats
- 1 c polenta or coarse cornmeal
- 1 flegg**
- ⅛ c dairy-free yogurt (coconut milk yogurt)
- 3 tbsp barbecue sauce (we used a pineapple, rum, and ginger sauce; think tangy and sweet)
- ¼ tsp of liquid smoke
- ½ tbsp cumin
- ½ tbsp paprika
- 1 tbsp chopped parsley
- salt and pepper to taste
- 2 tbsp ketchup

Recipe:

- Preheat oven to 350º F.; grease 5x9 loaf pan with olive oil.
- Prepare dry lentils; cook down until all the water has been soaked up and lentils are like a paste.
- Prepare flegg and allow it to gel in the fridge while you are cooking the lentils.
- In the food processor, chop the celery, onion, carrot, and garlic. Add minced mushrooms and sweat over medium heat. Remove from heat and let cool.
- In the food processor, add black beans and instant oats. Roughly chop with two or three pulses. Add the beans and oats to the veggie mixture; mix well.
- Once the lentils are cooked, take about ¾ of them and puree in the food processor until smooth. Add the puree and the whole lentils to the bean-and-veggie mix.
- Add in parsley, yogurt, cumin, paprika, liquid smoke, barbecue sauce, and walnuts.
- Add in flegg; top with polenta, and mix well to combine. Taste and season with salt and pepper to your liking!
- Bake for 40 minutes at 350º F. Top with ketchup and return to oven.
- Bake for another 10 minutes.
- Let sit for 15 minutes before slicing to serve.

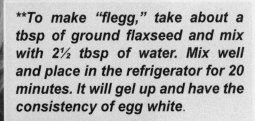

To make "flegg," take about a tbsp of ground flaxseed and mix with 2½ tbsp of water. Mix well and place in the refrigerator for 20 minutes. It will gel up and have the consistency of egg white.

We served the loaf with vegan mashed potatoes and a vegan mushroom gravy.

Loaftover 1: **The Kentucky Not Brown**

- Take a healthy slice of the Neatloaf and dredge it in egg and flour twice like you would for fried chicken.
- Fry in oil over high heat.
- Serve open-faced on toast with cheese and a fried egg.

Loaftover 2: **The Faloafel**

We used our air fryer for this one, which gave these a nice crisp without the oil, but you can bake or pan-fry these as well.

- Form small ¼ c-sized patties of the leftover loaf mixture.
- Roll in cornmeal to coat.
- Fry any way you feel like.
- Serve with cucumber/yogurt/dill sauce inside a warm pita.

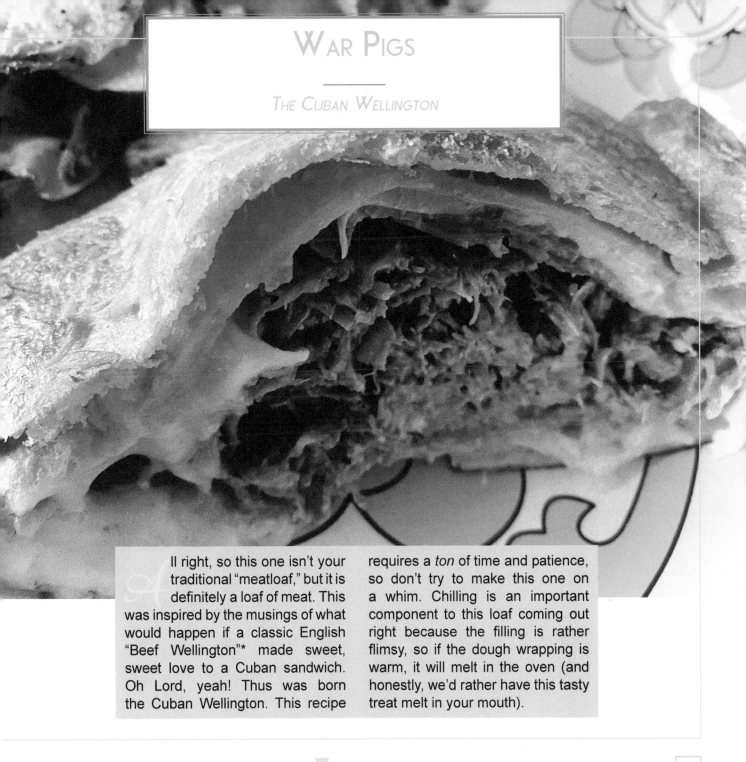

WAR PIGS

THE CUBAN WELLINGTON

All right, so this one isn't your traditional "meatloaf," but it is definitely a loaf of meat. This was inspired by the musings of what would happen if a classic English "Beef Wellington"* made sweet, sweet love to a Cuban sandwich. Oh Lord, yeah! Thus was born the Cuban Wellington. This recipe requires a *ton* of time and patience, so don't try to make this one on a whim. Chilling is an important component to this loaf coming out right because the filling is rather flimsy, so if the dough wrapping is warm, it will melt in the oven (and honestly, we'd rather have this tasty treat melt in your mouth).

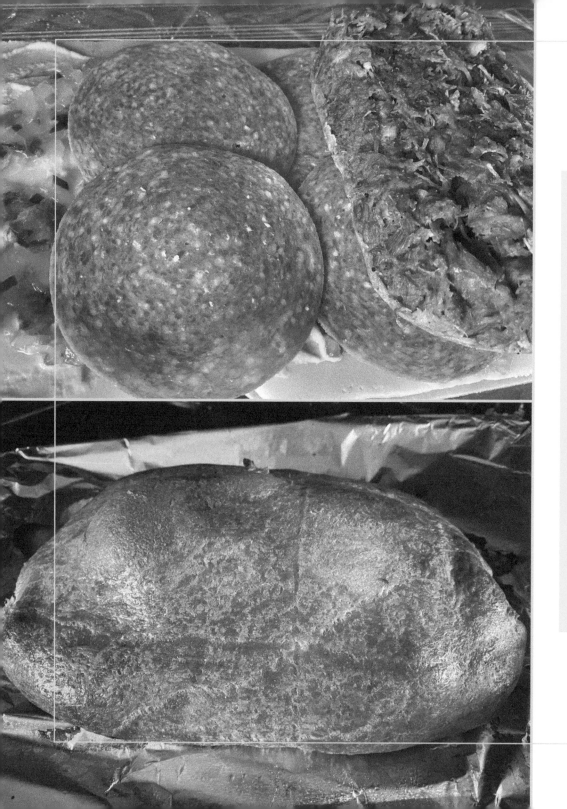

Ingredients:

For pulled pork:

- 1 lb pork shoulder
- ¼ tsp salt
- ¼ tsp onion powder
- ⅛ tsp black pepper
- ⅛ tsp garlic powder
- 1 c chicken/beef broth

For loaf:

- 1 lb of cooked pulled pork
- ½ lb sliced ham
- ½ lb sliced Swiss cheese
- ½ lb sliced salami
- 2 tbsp yellow mustard
- 4 tbsp relish
- 2 cans crescent rolls
- 1 egg, lightly beaten
- 2 tbsp milk

Recipe:

- Make 1 lb of pulled pork in slow cooker or Instant Pot.

To make the pork in the Instant Pot:

(Alternately, you can use a slow cooker for 4 hours on HIGH; just sear the pork in a cast-iron pan first.)

- Trim fat from pork roast.
- Cut into even chunks.
- In a large bowl, mix the dry ingredients; then rub pork with the mix and coat well.
- In the Instant Pot, add a little bit of olive oil and set to sauté.
- Once the Instant Pot is hot, add the seasoned pork.
- Sear for 3-5 minutes per side; then remove from Instant Pot.
- Press cancel and add chicken broth to Instant Pot.
- Deglaze the bottom with a spoon.
- Place pork back into the Instant Pot, secure lid, and pressure-cook for 60 minutes.
- Let pressure release naturally for 20 minutes before opening.

- Remove pork from the cooker and shred. Add 1-2 slices of Swiss cheese to help hold the meat together. Let cool, then form into a log-shaped patty. Place in the refrigerator to cool completely.
- When the pulled pork loaf is solid, you can build the remainder of the Wellington.
- Lay out a sheet of plastic wrap to help you roll the loaf. Layer on the ham, Swiss cheese, salami, mustard, and relish. Set the pulled pork loaf in the center and roll the wrapping around it tightly using the plastic wrap. Seal off the edges and place in the refrigerator to chill.
- Lay another sheet of plastic wrap. Spread out 2 cans of Pillsbury Crescent Rolls dough (or any other puff pastry-type wrapping). Place the chilled and wrapped pork loaf in the center and wrap the dough tightly around the meat. Keep wrapped in plastic and place in the refrigerator to chill at least 1 hour up to overnight.
- Preheat oven to 400º F.
- Prepare a baking sheet or loaf pan with light cooking spray. Brush the tops and sides of loaf with beaten egg and milk wash.
- Bake in the oven for 30 minutes. Let sit for 10 minutes before cutting and serving

*Rabbit-hole alert: No one really seems to know where the Beef Wellington originated. Some say it's a traditional African dish made with goat meat; some say Julia Child invented it in France in the 1970s; some say the Duke of Wellington created it. Either way, it's pretty popular in England *now* so we're going with that.*

M-m-m-my Samosa

The Indian Loaf

ell, clearly we've got the Knack for making good meatloaf. This loaf got its inspiration from an Indian food takeout night. We had gotten chicken korma and saag channa, which ended up just tasting so darn good all mixed together, so we took all the components of those two dishes and melded them together to create this loaf. The unique item in this loaf is the jhal muri, which is a traditional Indian street food snack (it's kind of like an Indian version of a popular American snack cracker party mix). It's made with puffed rice, roasted peanuts, spices, and mustard oil. We didn't make our own because we had ordered it with the takeout food and had extra! It is available for purchase premade, or you can get adventurous and make your own. We do highly recommend seeking this product out, as it truly added an extra kick of Indian spices.

Ingredients:

- 1 lb ground chicken
- 1 lb ground lamb
- 1 onion — diced
- ½ 14.5 oz can diced tomatoes
- 2 tsp + 1 tsp garam masala
- 2 handfuls of baby spinach — roughly chopped
- 1 15.5 oz can chickpeas — roughly chopped
- 2 tsp paprika
- 1 tsp curry powder
- 1 tsp turmeric
- 1 tsp salt
- ¼ tsp garlic powder
- ¼ c Greek yogurt
- 14 oz korma sauce
- 1 egg
- 1½ c jhal muri

Recipe:
- Preheat oven to 350º F.; grease 5x9 loaf pan with butter.

In the food processor:
- Chop the jhal muri to a fine grind; set aside.
- Pulse diced tomatoes and onions together.
- Pulse spinach and chickpeas together.

For the loaf:
- Sauté onion and tomatoes over medium heat to reduce slightly. Add 2 tsp of garam masala and sauté until fragrant.
- Add in spinach and chickpeas and mix until spinach is just wilted. Cool to room temperature.
- In large bowl, mix by hand chicken and lamb.

- Add in the remaining garam masala, paprika, curry powder, turmeric, salt, garlic powder, and yogurt. Mix until well combined.
- Add ¾ of the cooled veggie mixture; save enough to top the loaf.
- Add in 3 tbsp of korma sauce to the loaf; then add 1 tbsp to the remaining veggie mixture. Set the remaining veggies aside.
- Crack in egg at room temperature to the loaf. Top with crushed jhal muri and combine.
- Bake for 45 minutes at 350º F. Top with veggie-and-sauce mix.
- Bake for another 10 minutes. Check internal temp to be 160º F.
- Let sit for 15 minutes before slicing to serve.

We served over steamed basmati rice and slathered with the remaining warmed korma sauce.

The loaftover: Samosas! Whip up a batch of dough and wrap up the remainder of this loaf for some warm, fried meat pockets. We'd never made samosas before, so we relied on our good friend YouTube to show us how to properly fold and fill them. We used the air fryer to cook them, and while they were delicious, they felt a little too healthy, so if you decide to make this loaftover, we recommend frying in oil!

Mama Mia-tloaf*

The Eastern European Loaf

For Olga and Barb, our mamas

y, my, how could we resist making this loaf?! The story behind this one is personal for both of us — an homage to both of our mothers, on various levels. The meatloaf itself is reminiscent of comfort, home, and family. The flavors of this loaf highlight the types of comfort food we both grew up with. Both of us come from an Eastern European background, Tom's family being Ukrainian and Kristen's family being Polish (among some other nationalities as well!). After doing some bare-minimum research, we stumbled on the stuffed cabbage roll, a dish that makes an appearance in almost every Eastern European country. We married the traditional recipes for the Ukrainian "holubtsi" and the Polish "golumpki" for this flavor-packed loaf. Because of the addition of the cured meats, this is a fattier loaf than most and doesn't require any extra salt.

Ingredients:

- 1¼ lb ground beef
- ½ lb ground kielbasa sausage (about 4 links)**
- ¼ lb ground bacon (about 8 strips)**
- ½ onion — diced
- ¼ head of cabbage — shredded
- 1 carrot — shredded
- 3 tbsp tomato soup + remainder for topping
- 1 tsp marjoram
- 1 tsp garlic powder
- ½ tsp nutmeg
- 1 tsp black pepper
- ¼ c sour cream
- 1½ c cooked and cooled white rice
- ½ c breadcrumbs
- 1 egg

Recipe:

- Preheat oven to 350° F.; grease 5x9 loaf pan with butter.
- Sauté onion, cabbage, and carrot until cabbage is wilted; cool to room temperature.
- In large bowl, mix by hand ground beef, ground bacon, and ground sausage.
- Add in the marjoram, garlic powder, pepper, and nutmeg. Mix until well combined.
- Add the cooled veggies and mix.
- Stir in 3 tbsp of tomato soup and sour cream.
- Crack in egg at room temperature and top with white rice and breadcrumbs. Mix until well combined.
- Bake for 40 minutes at 350° F. Top with remaining tomato soup.
- Bake for another 10 minutes. Check internal temp to be 160° F.
- Let sit for 25 minutes before slicing to serve.

We served the loaf with pan-roasted beets and cucumber dill salad.

Before you send us an angry tweet, yes we know that ABBA is Swedish, but guess what? Sweden also has a strikingly similar stuffed cabbage dish called "kaldomar." And the whole point of this book is to combine cultures, happily. So shut up. Also, good luck finding us on Twitter; we don't twit.

**We purchased kielbasa and bacon and ground them together in the meat grinder to match the consistency of the ground beef. You could probably use your food processor for a similar result. Don't forget to remove the casings from your sausage!*

Loaftovers: Pierogi!

Loaf You Madly

The Dessert Loaf

A Play in One Act:

Tom: We should totally make a dessert loaf!
Kristen: Ooooohh! Great idea! Like a mincemeat kinda thing?
Tom: No, like it'll be sweet bread and icing and stuff.
Kristen: That's cake. You just described a cake.

Ingredients:

- Sense of humor
- Boxed cake mix
- Store-bought icing

Recipe:

- Preheat oven to 350° F.
- Pop that cake batter in a loaf pan.
- Bake for 40 minutes.
- Let cool before icing.
- Let the meat cake.

THREE LITTLE BIRDS

The Turducken Loaf

ere we go being all extra again … but every little thing is gonna be all right once you try this tryptophan triptych.

This loaf definitely started as a joke, but the more we thought about it, the more we realized we could pull this off and make a meatloaf that had an ENTIRE Thanksgiving meal in it from the turkey on down to the cranberries. It literally has everything in it except your drunk family member asking, "When'r'you getting a REEEAL job?"

Each of these loaves needs to be made separately and then cooled for at least an hour in the fridge so they are better able to be formed into the shape you want. This is another all-day event, much like making a Thanksgiving dinner, so make sure you have the time to dedicate to building this beautiful loaf.

Ingredients:

Chicken loaf:
- 1 lb ground chicken
- ½ c boxed stuffing mix, ground in food processor
- ¼ c cream of mushroom soup
- ½ egg (~1 oz)
- 1 celery rib — diced
- ¼ white onion — diced
- ½ tsp black pepper
- ½ tsp ground mustard
- 2 tsp chili sauce

Duck loaf:
- 1 lb ground duck*
- ½ c plain breadcrumbs
- 2 tbsp cream of mushroom soup
- ½ egg (~1 oz)
- ¼ c carrot — shredded
- ¼ c dried cranberries — chopped
- ¼ tsp pumpkin pie spice
- ½ tsp rubbed sage
- ¼ tsp onion powder
- 1 tsp tomato paste
- pinch of salt

Turkey loaf
- 1 lb ground turkey
- ½ c boxed stuffing mix, ground in food processor
- ¼ c cream of mushroom soup
- ½ egg (~1 oz)
- ¼ white onion — diced
- ½ can green beans — chopped
- pinch of salt

Sweet Potatoes
- 2 medium sweet potatoes — peeled and diced
- ¼ c milk
- 2 tbsp butter
- 2 tbsp cream of mushroom soup
- 2 tsp pumpkin pie spice
- 1 tsp salt
- ½ c candied walnuts — chopped

Recipe:

- Grease 5x9 loaf pan with butter and put in the fridge while you make the loaves; the colder everything is, the better.

Make the chicken loaf:

- Sauté the onion and celery until just wilted.
- In large mixing bowl, mix all ingredients by hand.
- Stir in sautéed onions and celery.
- Spread out onto a wax paper-covered sheet pan and put in the fridge.

Make the duck loaf:

- None of the ingredients are cooked; just mix all of them together in a large mixing bowl.
- Spread out onto a wax paper-covered sheet pan and put in the fridge.

Make the turkey loaf:

- Sauté the onion and green beans until just wilted.
- In a large mixing bowl, mix all ingredients by hand.
- Stir in sautéed onion and green beans.
- Spread out onto a wax paper-covered sheet pan and put in the fridge.

Once all the loaves have been made and have chilled for about an hour, they are ready to be molded.

- Preheat oven to 350° F.
- Remove the chilled loaf pan from the fridge.
- Layer in the turkey loaf on the long sides and the bottom; be careful to save about a quarter of the mix because you will need it to top the loaf.
- Layer in the duck loaf in the same fashion, but don't go all the way up the sides because you're going to top the whole thing with the turkey.
- Place a log of the chicken loaf in the center; you will have some extra of this loaf.
- Cover the chicken with a thin layer of the duck loaf.
- Cover the whole pan with a thin layer of the turkey loaf.
- Place loaf in the preheated oven for 50 minutes.
- While loaf is cooking, make mashed sweet potatoes.

For the sweet potatoes:

- Bring diced potatoes to a boil until fork-tender (about 20 minutes).
- Drain potatoes and beat in milk, butter, spices, and cream of mushroom soup.
- Stir in candied walnuts.

Back the to loaf:

- After the loaf has cooked for 50 minutes, top with mashed sweet potatoes and return to the oven for 10 minutes. Check internal temperature to be 160° F.
- Let cool for 15 minutes before slicing to serve.

We served the loaf with brown gravy and remaining potatoes (or whatever Thanksgiving fixin's strike you!).

If you can't find ground duck, you can always butcher and grind a whole duck like a maniac.

he following are ideas that never quite made it into the book because they were either impossible or too ridiculous. And if you've made it this far, you know we didn't shy away from doing ridiculous things. It's probably for the best that we had *some* standards.

I AIN'T AFRAID OF NO LOAF

Made with ghost meat.

HIGHER LOAF

Whatever the oil component was would've been made with cannabis. Steve Winwood was involved.

TAINTED LOAF

Made with rotten meat.

SILENCE OF THE LOAVES

Made with human meat (or ground liver), fava beans, and a nice Chianti.

CHARLOAF'S WEB

Spider meat.

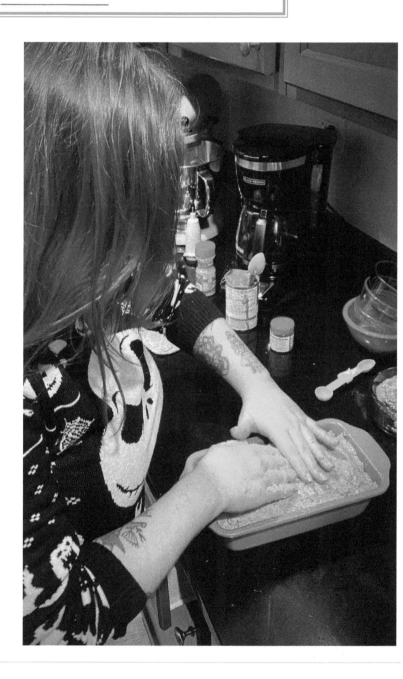

CPSIA information can be obtained
at www.ICGtesting.com
Printed in the USA
LVHW070855160321
681666LV00016B/390